AF228596

BOARD GAMES
MILTON BRADLEY

Lee Slater

Big Buddy Books

An Imprint of Abdo Publishing
abdobooks.com

abdobooks.com

Published by Abdo Publishing, a division of ABDO, PO Box 398166, Minneapolis, Minnesota 55439.
Copyright © 2022 by Abdo Consulting Group, Inc. International copyrights reserved in all countries.
No part of this book may be reproduced in any form without written permission from the publisher.
Big Buddy Books™ is a trademark and logo of Abdo Publishing.

Printed in the United States of America, North Mankato, Minnesota
102021
012022

THIS BOOK CONTAINS RECYCLED MATERIALS

Design: Emily O'Malley, Mighty Media, Inc.
Production: Mighty Media, Inc.
Editor: Liz Salzmann
Cover Photographs: Andronos Haris/Shutterstock Images (money), Buturlimov Pavlo/Shutterstock Images (dog), de2marco/Shutterstock Images (game pieces), digitalreflections/Shutterstock Images (Candy Land), julie deshaies/Shutterstock Images (Battleship), Leila Alekto Photo/Shutterstock Images (dice), Wikimedia Commons (Bradley)
Interior Photographs: C.W. Bardeen/Wikimedia Commons, p. 17; Courtesy of The Strong®, Rochester, New York, p. 21; digidreamgrafix/Shutterstock Images, p. 25; digitalreflections/Shutterstock Images, pp. 27, 29 (top); Everett Collection/Shutterstock Images, p. 9; Granger, p. 11; Jiri Hera/Shutterstock Images, pp. 19, 29 (bottom); Library of Congress, pp. 15, 28 (right); Old Paper Studios/Alamy Photo, p. 23; TonelsonProductions/Shutterstock Images, p. 13; Tupungato/Shutterstock Images, pp. 7, 28 (left); Wangkun Jia/Shutterstock Images, p. 5

Library of Congress Control Number: 2021942813

Publisher's Cataloging-in-Publication Data
Names: Slater, Lee, author.
Title: Board games: Milton Bradley / by Lee Slater
Description: Minneapolis, Minnesota : Abdo Publishing, 2022 | Series: Toy stories | Includes online resources and index.
Identifiers: ISBN 9781532197086 (lib. bdg.) | ISBN 9781098219215 (ebook)
Subjects: LCSH: Bradley, Milton, 1836-1911--Juvenile literature. | Board games--Juvenile literature. | Inventors--Juvenile literature. | Toys--Juvenile literature. | Milton Bradley Company--Juvenile literature.
Classification: DDC 338.47688--dc23

CONTENTS

WORK & PLAY

Milton Bradley was born on November 8, 1836, in Vienna, Maine. He grew up in Lowell, Massachusetts.

Milton's father showed Milton how to use objects such as apples to solve math problems. This made homework feel more like play than work. Milton continued to mix work and play for the rest of his life.

Lowell, Massachusetts, the city where Milton spent his childhood

CHAPTER 2

SCHOOL DAYS

Bradley graduated from Lowell High School in 1854. That fall, he started studying **drafting** at the Lawrence Scientific School at Harvard University.

However, before Bradley could finish, his parents moved to Hartford, Connecticut. Bradley went with them. He never finished college.

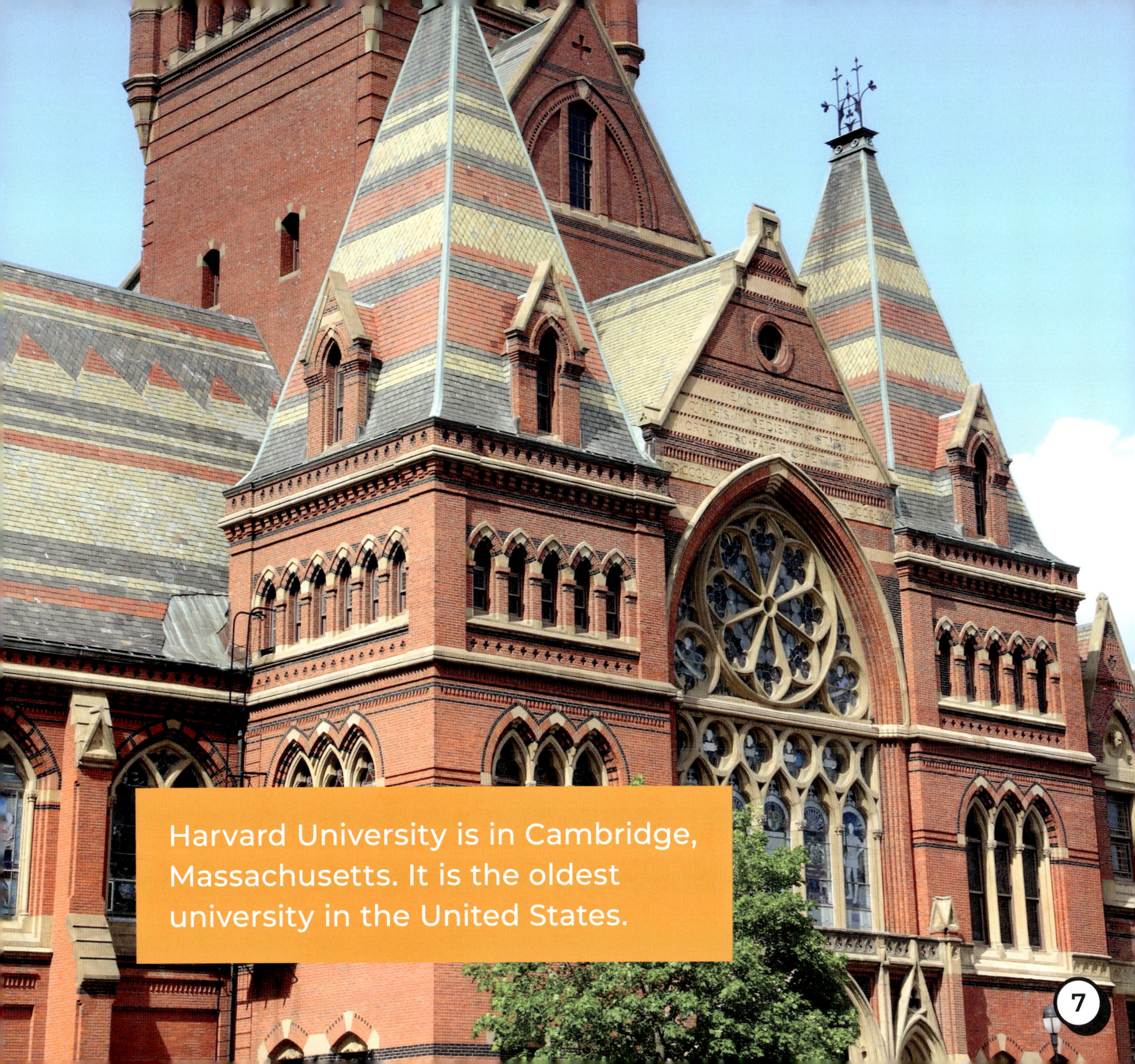

Harvard University is in Cambridge, Massachusetts. It is the oldest university in the United States.

EARLY CAREER

In 1856, Bradley got a job at the Wason Manufacturing Company in Springfield, Massachusetts. It manufactured train cars.

At work, Bradley saw a **lithograph**. It inspired him to learn lithography. He used this skill to start the Milton Bradley Company in 1860. It printed **items** for local businesses.

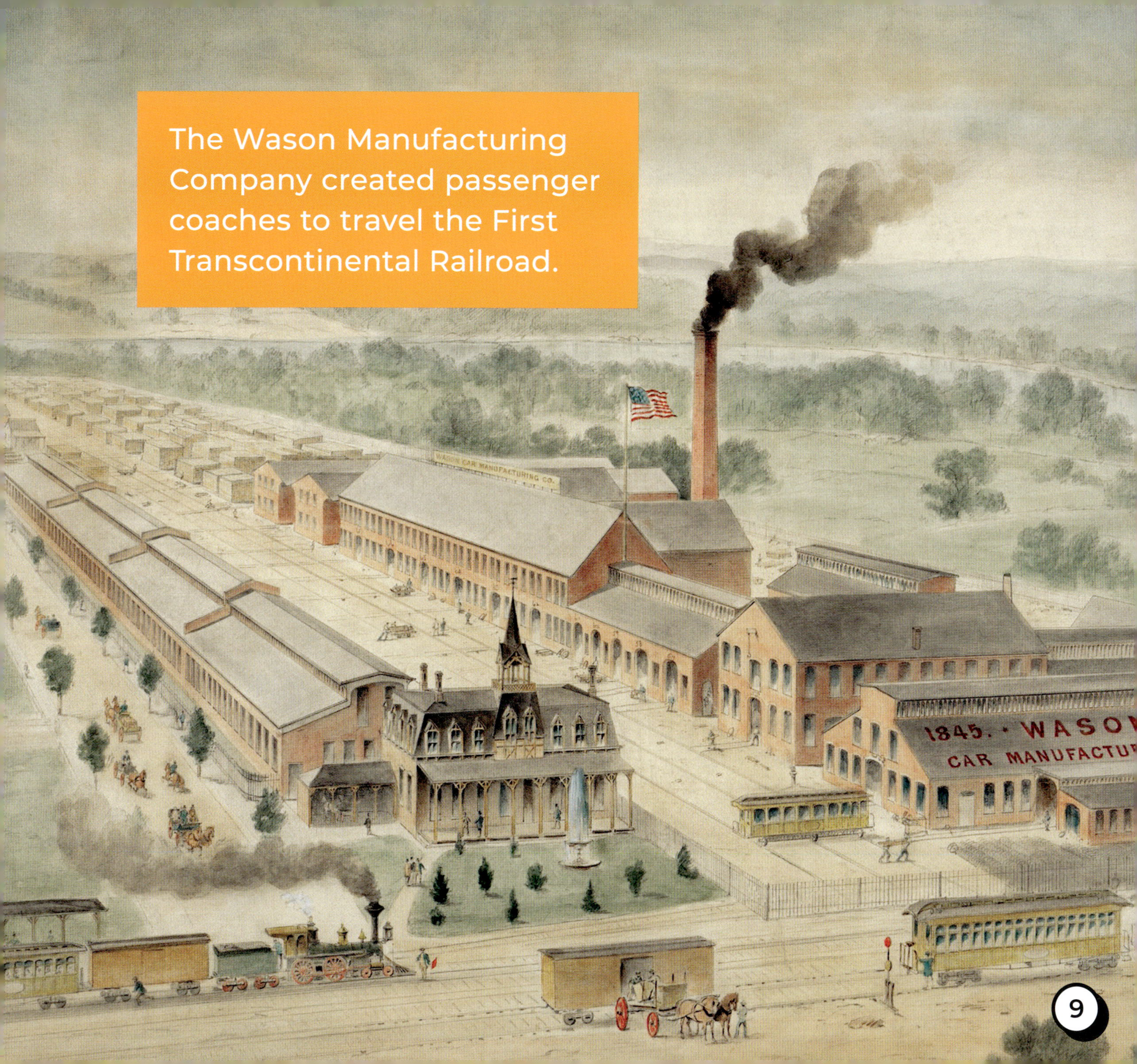

The Wason Manufacturing Company created passenger coaches to travel the First Transcontinental Railroad.

9

CHAPTER 4

FIRST GAME

During the summer of 1860, Bradley decided to make a board game. Bradley called his game The Checkered Game of Life. The **theme** was the ups and downs of life. The game was a success!

Bradley was also successful in his personal life. Near the end of 1860, he married Vilona Larue Eaton.

THE CHECKERED GAME OF LIFE.

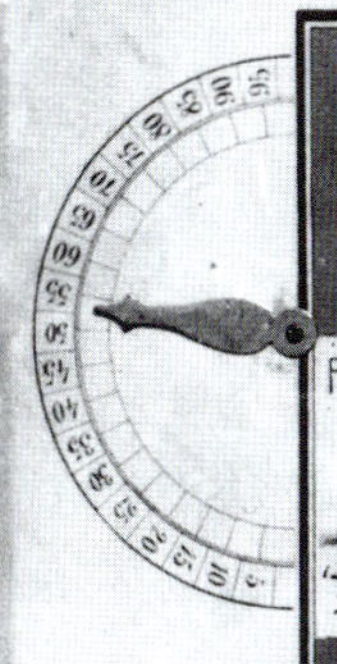

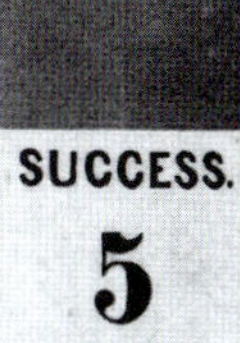

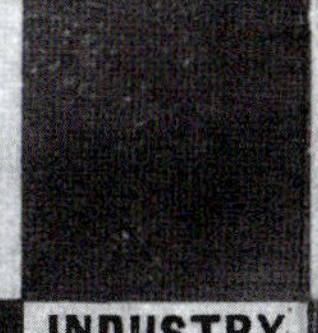

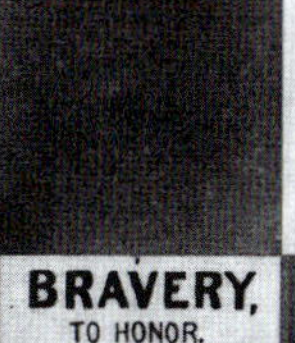

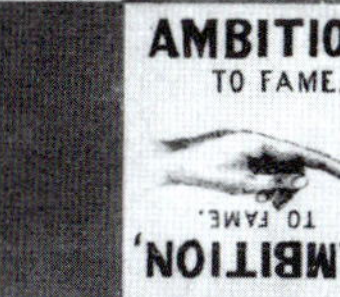
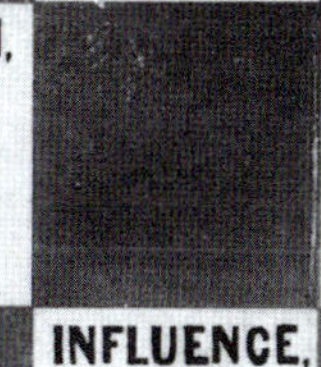

Bradley's original game board

CHAPTER 5

MAKING A GAME

Every board game starts with an idea. Then the game creator makes a **prototype**. The prototype is tested and changed based on advice from players.

Then a factory makes the game boards and pieces. The games are put in boxes and shipped to stores, where people buy them. At home, the new game is opened, and the fun begins!

Today, thousands of
new board games are
published each year.

CHAPTER 6

WAR EFFORT

The **Civil War** began in 1861. During the war, Bradley used his **drafting** skills to **design** weapons. He also created a game kit to raise soldiers' **morale**.

Near the end of the war, J.F. Tapley and Clark W. Bryan became Bradley's business partners. After the war ended in 1865, the three men returned to creating board games.

Soldiers relax in their barracks. Bradley's game kit was a much-needed distraction in difficult times.

 REAL LIFE

Bradley continued to have success in business. But sadly, his wife, Vilona, died in 1867. Two years later, Bradley married teacher Ellen "Nellie" Thayer.

That year, he learned about German kindergartens. Kindergartens used creative activities to help children learn. Bradley wanted to bring kindergarten to the United States.

Educator Friedrich Froebel led the German kindergarten movement.

KINDERGARTEN

In 1869, Bradley added educational supplies to the company's products. These included blocks and art supplies.

Bradley traveled the country to show teachers his educational supplies. He often gave them away to encourage opening kindergartens. Bradley and Nellie started the first kindergarten in Springfield.

Modern toy blocks
are very similar to the
ones Bradley made.

CHAPTER 9

HARD TIMES

In the 1870s, the United States was in a **recession**. Bradley's company struggled to stay profitable. His **investors** were worried. They wanted Bradley to stop giving away supplies. But Bradley wouldn't do that.

So, Tapley bought the investors' **shares**. He also became company president.

In 1880, Milton Bradley Company produced its first jigsaw puzzle, the Smashed Up Locomotive.

CHAPTER 10

NEW OPPORTUNITIES

Bradley saw that art supplies were too expensive for many schools to purchase. So, he created inexpensive paints and crayons for schools.

Bradley also wanted his supplies to be easy to get. His company was one of the first to sell its products through the mail.

Bradley also published magazines for teachers that contained news, stories, and advertisements.

CHAPTER 11

THE END GAME

Bradley retired from the Milton Bradley Company in 1906. But he continued to **contribute** new ideas.

Milton Bradley died on May 11, 1911. His life's work was done, but he would never be forgotten. His name has become **synonymous** with great board games.

Milton Bradley Company
will always have a place
in Springfield's history.

BRADLEY'S LEGACY

Hasbro continues to produce games created by Milton Bradley. These games delight children and adults. The games also support Bradley's vision for people to have fun together.

Bradley's **imagination** and **passion** made a lasting **contribution**. People around the world can enjoy the result of his inventions and accomplishments.

Candy Land is just one of Milton Bradley Company's classic games.

TIMELINE

1836

Milton Bradley is born on November 8 in Vienna, Maine.

1860

Bradley founds the Milton Bradley Company and creates The Checkered Game of Life. He marries Vilona Larue Eaton.

1854

Bradley studies drafting at Harvard.

1861

The Civil War begins. Milton Bradley Company produces a game kit for soldiers.

1867

Bradley's wife, Vilona, dies.

1869

Bradley becomes interested in the kindergarten movement. Milton Bradley Company begins producing educational supplies. Bradley marries Ellen "Nellie" Thayer.

1906

Bradley retires from Milton Bradley Company.

1911

Milton Bradley dies on May 11.

GLOSSARY

Civil War—the war between the United States of America and the Confederate States of America from 1861 to 1865.

contribute (kahn-TRIB-yoot)—to give help to accomplish a goal.

design (dih-ZINE)—to plan how something will appear or work.

drafting—a job that involves making detailed drawings and plans for things such as machines and structures.

imagination—the creative ability to think up new ideas and form mental images of things that aren't real or present.

investor—someone who gives money to a company in return for part of the company's profits.

item—an individual thing.

lithograph—a picture created through the process of printing from a smooth, flat stone or a metal plate. On this surface, the picture or the design holds printing ink. The rest of the surface does not.

morale—the enthusiasm and loyalty a person or group feels about a task or job.

passion—a strong feeling about something or someone.

prototype—an original model on which something is patterned.

recession—a period of time when business activity slows.

share—one of the equal parts into which the ownership of a company is divided.

synonymous—strongly suggesting a particular idea, person, or quality is closely associated with something.

theme—the main subject of something such as a book, movie, or game.

INDEX